Taking Action

Support for Families of Children with Sexual Behavior Problems

Jane F. Silovsky, Ph.D.

Brandon, Vermont

Publication made possible by a generous grant from the Florence V. Burden Foundation.

Copyright © 2009 by the Safer Society Press, Brandon, Vermont

First Edition

All rights reserved. No part of this book may be reproduced in any form or by any electronic or mechanical means, including information storage and retrieval systems, without permission in writing from the publisher, except by a reviewer who may quote brief passages.

ISBN: 978-1-884444-80-7

Printed in the United States of America

10 9 8 7 6 5 4 3 2 1

P.O. Box 340
Brandon, VT 05733
www.safersociety.org
(802) 247-3132

Safer Society Press is a program of the Safer Society Foundation, a 501(C)3 nonprofit dedicated to the prevention and treatment of sexual abuse. For more information, visit our Web site at www.safersociety.org.

Taking Action: Support for Families of Children with Sexual Behavior Problems

$5.00 plus shipping and handling (bulk discounts available)

Order # WP136

DEDICATION AND ACKNOWLEDGMENTS

This booklet is dedicated to the parents and caregivers who have cared for children with sexual behavior problems with whom I have had the pleasure to work and learn. I admire your fortitude, willingness to try new parenting behaviors, and love for your children.

I wish to acknowledge the teachings of Barbara Bonner, Bill Friedrich, Mark Chaffin, and Lucy Berliner, as well as the feedback and insights from my reviewers, clinic team members, and editors at Safer Society, Marjorie Ryerson and Gaen Murphree.

CONTENTS

Publisher's Note, vii

Introduction, ix

ONE
Definitions and Responses, 1

TWO
Background Information about Sexual Development and Sexual Behavior Problems, 5

THREE
How Do Children Develop Sexual Behavior Problems?, 18

FOUR
Taking Action: Safety Planning for Children with Sexual Behavior Problems, 24

FIVE
Taking Action: Finding the Right Treatment for Children with Sexual Behavior Problems and Their Families, 39

SIX
Taking Action: Advocating for Children with Sexual Behavior Problems, 55

SEVEN
Placement and Reunification, 61

EIGHT
Taking Action: Taking Care of Yourself, 66

Resources, 69

PUBLISHER'S NOTE

This guidebook is written for you—parents and caregivers who have learned their child has a sexual behavior problem and who want to understand and help change that behavior.

At this point, and over the next several months, the most important thing you can do is help your child as he or she faces the challenge of developing new, healthier behaviors. That's where *Taking Action* comes in. Written by one of the leading authorities in the field, this guidebook provides the information you will need to support your child and access the resources you and your child will require in the days to come.

Preparation and publication of *Taking Action: Support for Families of Children with Sexual Behavior Problems* was funded by the Florence V. Burden Foundation. We are indebted to them for their support of this book and their recognition that early intervention in the troubling behaviors of adolescents and children is one of the best ways to prevent problems in adulthood and to create a safer society.

The Safer Society Foundation, Inc., is a private, nonprofit agency with a 30-year heritage of working to end sexual abuse and its harmful effects on families and our society. To learn more about Safer Society visit our Web site at www.safersociety.org.

INTRODUCTION

Having a child who acts out sexually is terribly stressful for any parent. Our children are flooded with sexual messages from the media (television, movies, music videos, lyrics of songs, and the Internet). Yet, sex remains a topic that can be embarrassing and hard for parents to discuss, particularly with their own children. Parenting classes and books rarely address sexual behaviors in children. So when inappropriate sexual behavior by a child is discovered, families often respond to the news with shock. They frequently lack information and adequate support to deal with the events surrounding identified problems with their child's sexual behavior.

This booklet is specifically designed to help parents and other caregivers of children (ages 3 to 12) who have sexual behavior problems. If you are reading this booklet, you may be a family member of a child who has acted out in a sexual manner. You also may be a friend or professional who wants to provide support. This booklet is designed to address many of the questions caregivers have about sexual behavior in children. Our goal is to help you develop a plan of action and to offer you hope for the future, for both you and your child.

Parents often feel ashamed and isolated after discovering that their child has a sexual behavior problem. If you find yourself in this place, it is important for you to know that you are not alone. It can be helpful to learn from other families in similar circumstances.

Four Families' Stories

Below are four examples of sexual behaviors in children and some of the questions and concerns that can arise for the parents and other family members as a result.

Example 1
Mr. and Mrs. Cornelison's four sons ranged in age from 5 to 10 years old. All the boys loved sports. Every evening and weekend was filled

with practices, games, and other activities. One Saturday morning, Mrs. Cornelison told her sons to get in their uniforms for their games. As the children dressed, it was unusually quiet in the bedroom, so Mrs. Cornelison went to see what was happening. She found two of her sons, ages 7 and 9, undressed and touching each other's private parts. She was shocked. She told her husband what she saw. Mr. Cornelison had the boys get dressed, and he talked to each of them separately. The boys seemed embarrassed. They reported that they were just getting dressed and were wondering what it would be like to touch each other.

The Cornelisons wondered if this behavior was normal or something of concern. If it was normal, should they just ignore it? What did this discovery mean about their boys and about their own parenting? What did this mean about how the boys would be when they grew up? Did this mean that their sons were gay?

Example 2
Mr. McFarland will never forget the night his neighbor called about his 10-year-old son, Ryan. Ryan had been at the neighbor's house playing with his friends, ages 9 and 6. The boys all got along well and played together often. When the neighbor called she sounded in a panic. She said that she had walked into the boys' bedroom, and had found them all half naked, with Ryan humping her 6-year-old son, Benjamin. In the next few months there were police investigations, child protective services involvement, and various other services that had been recommended by the authorities. At first, Mr. McFarland didn't or couldn't believe it had happened. He thought the neighbor had misinterpreted how the boys were playing. Then, over time, he accepted that the sexual behaviors had really occurred.

Many questions arose for Mr. McFarland throughout this process. For example, where had Ryan learned this behavior? Had Ryan himself been sexually abused? Was he going to grow up to be a pedophile? What rights would the family have in the investigation process? What kinds of treatment could help Ryan?

Example 3

Ms. Blackwood is worried about her grandchildren, Summer, age 7, and Darren, age 5. Their father sexually abused them a year ago. Summer and Darren were sent to live with Ms. Blackwood after her daughter (the children's mother) left to be with her husband. Since being in her home, her grandchildren seem to have no boundaries. No one is a stranger to them. They try to hug or kiss everyone. Summer especially likes to talk with men, even at the grocery store. Recently, Ms. Blackwood found Summer with her mouth on Darren's privates while they were taking a bath together. Ms. Blackwood didn't know what to do; she just froze watching them. After the initial state of shock, she told the children that they had better stop that. Summer wasn't upset about the behavior or about how it might impact Darren. Ms. Blackwood is afraid that Summer is becoming a "psychopath" and has no concern for others. At the same time, Ms. Blackwood doesn't want to punish Summer too harshly because of the past sexual abuse and loss of their mother. Ms. Blackwood worries that Summer will get really upset if she is punished and may be hurt by it.

Ms. Blackwood is unsure what to do. What should she do about the bathroom incident? What type of discipline is appropriate, if any? This situation is terribly stressful for Ms. Blackwood, but she doesn't think she can talk with anyone about what has happened. Who can she get help from when she feels all alone?

Example 4

Mr. and Mrs. Kastner adopted Jerry, age 10, and Destiny, age 5, two years ago. Jerry and Destiny had been removed from their biological parents' home due to neglect and physical abuse. Jerry had been more damaged by the past experiences than his younger sister. Over the time with the Kastners, Jerry has revealed that his biological parents and other adults often had fistfights and even sometimes hit Jerry. The parents also frequently got drunk or used drugs and left Jerry and Destiny to fend for themselves. While Destiny has adjusted well to the Kastner home, Jerry has had difficulties following rules. He tends to be angry at home and at school. He struggles with his schoolwork, and now is close to failing. Recently, a school administrator called and reported that Jerry and two other boys had held down a younger female student. When a teacher found the students, Jerry had his pants down and was lying on top of the girl. Jerry was suspended from school, and now the police have become involved. The psychologist who evaluated Jerry diagnosed him with a condition called Oppositional Defiant Disorder. Jerry was also found to have reading and math learning disabilities. She recommended that the family receive therapy and that Jerry be placed on a special education plan designed just for him, so that his learning and behavior problems could be addressed.

The Kastners are unsure what they can expect from therapy. They wonder if therapy can actually help Jerry and, if so, what type would be best. The wonder if they should be worried about Jerry doing something to Destiny. They care about Jerry but also are offended by his behavior. They want to know how to help themselves deal with their own negative reactions.

When a parent has a child who demonstrates sexual behavior problems, many questions arise such as the ones these parents have expressed. The families described in these examples are similar to the hundreds of families that we have supported in our clinic. In the following pages, these families' questions are addressed as well as other questions parents and caregivers may have.

In today's world, children are raised by multiple and varied caregivers, including not only biological parents, but also adoptive parents, stepparents, grandparents, aunts, uncles, older siblings, and foster parents. For simplicity's sake, we will use the terms "parents" and "caregivers" interchangeably throughout this booklet to mean those adults who are responsible for the care, nurturing, guidance, and raising of children.

This Booklet's Purpose

The information provided in this booklet comes from over a decade of work in our specialty clinic. Our clinic provides evaluations and therapy, and conducts research with preschool and school-age children with sexual behavior problems. All of our services integrate work with the families, as well. Researchers across the country have learned a lot over the last two decades about children who have sexual behavior problems. We now know more than ever about the causes and types of such behavior problems. More importantly, we have learned a great deal about what types of treatments help children with sexual behavior problems and their families. The best results happen when parents and other important adults learn how to help and provide the support needed for children with sexual behavior problems.

In this booklet, information about body parts and sexual behavior is described. Medical/technical terms for body parts (also called "anatomically detailed" terms) will be used to help clarify information and examples. Families from some cultures avoid technical terms for sexual body parts and use other terms instead. Some may prefer to use their native language rather than English terms for body parts. We decided to use technical terms in this booklet when details are required for clear understanding. The phrases "sexual body parts" and "private parts" are used when more specific terms are not required.

Because this booklet directly addresses sexual behavior of children, it may be distressing for some caregivers to read. In our work with families we have found it most helpful to directly address the issues and provide education. Treatments that have been found most helpful for children with sexual behavior problems also directly discuss and address these issues. The booklet was designed to be informative. Care was taken to present facts clearly but respectfully.

In addition to the four examples of families described earlier, we have included statements from other families throughout this booklet. The four families and the statements are not exact replications of real families or quotes from specific caregivers. We have done this to protect the anonymity of the actual families.

ONE

Definitions and Responses

What Is a Sexual Behavior Problem?

Many parents do not want to think about their children as sexual beings until they become young adults. However, sexual behavior may start as early as infancy. Parents of boys often talk about how their sons will touch themselves when their diapers are being changed. Children are curious. They are not only curious about their own bodies, but also about other people's bodies. Children's curiosity may even lead to touching each other's private parts or "playing doctor."

Sometimes, however, the sexual behaviors of children are more than a result of harmless curiosity. At times the sexual behavior of children becomes harmful to themselves and to other children. Guidelines now exist to help parents determine if the sexual behavior of their children is a problem. Parents should be concerned when their children's sexual acts or behaviors have one or more of the following characteristics:

- occur frequently (they happen a lot, not just every once in a while);
- take place between children of widely differing ages (such as a 12-year-old who acts out with a 4-year-old) or between children of different abilities;
- are initiated with strong, upset feelings, such as anger or anxiety;
- cause harm or potential harm (physical or emotional) to any child;
- do not respond to typical parenting strategies (such as discipline); or
- Involve coercion, force, or aggression of any kind.

Sexual behavior problems that are displayed by children are troubling. Such behaviors involve inappropriate or harmful use of sexual body parts, such as the buttocks, breasts, anus, or genitals (including the penis, vulva, and vagina). The child displaying the sexual behavior as well as any other children who might have been witness to it, or who might have been involved, may be harmed by such behavior.

Different types of sexual behavior problems include

- a child who sexually touches him or herself, causing physical harm or damage (such as touching one's own private parts so much that they become red and sore);
- a child who often wants to look at other people when they have no clothes on (such as looking underneath the bathroom stall at other children);
- sexual interactions with other children that range from inappropriate touching (without permission) to intercourse; and
- sexual behaviors that involve force or aggression. These are of greatest concern, particularly when they occur between children with large differences in their ages.

While adults who sexually abuse children are motivated by sexual urges, it is very different for children. In contrast to adult sex offenders, the sexual behaviors of children usually take place for other reasons, such as when a child feels anxious or angry, is reacting to a traumatic experience, is overly curious after seeing sexual materials, seeks attention, is trying to imitate others, or is merely trying to calm him or herself.

Sexual behavior problems in children are not limited to any particular group of children or gender. Sexual behavior problems occur in children across age ranges, socioeconomic (income) levels, cultural groups, living circumstances, and family structures. Some children with sexual behavior problems have parents who are married, some have parents who are divorced. Some have abuse histories, some have no history of abuse or other trauma. But they are all children first. They are children who have shown a behavior that is not acceptable and that needs treatment.

Initial Responses by Parents and Caregivers

When parents first discover that their child has a sexual behavior problem, the parents may have many different reactions. No initial response is "right" or "wrong." There are no clearly defined "stages" that parents go through. Common reactions by parents include

- difficulty believing that the sexual behavior really occurred;
- anger or blame at their child, at the other child, at themselves as parents, at the world, or at the person who abused the child (if that occurred);
- negative feelings toward their child or withdrawal from their own child;
- sadness and depression;
- guilt or remorse;
- shame;
- a sense of feeling alone and/or isolated;
- disappointment, because the child could have made better choices;
- confusion and uncertainty, especially when the child does not have a history of being sexually abused (not knowing where the sexual behavior has come from can be quite upsetting for caregivers); and
- distress, nightmares, and general discomfort, particularly when the parent has been sexually abused as a child. (Memories of their own past abuse can come to the surface and can affect how parents see their children and how they then react.)

When you find yourself in this situation, with the right support systems you *can* move from distress to a sense of hope and to a better future. It is important for you to know that you are not alone. Other parents have experienced very similar emotions and reactions to yours.

It can help to know that sexual behaviors in children typically lessen with the right type of treatment and when families are actively involved in services. Through such treatments, future sexual behavior problems can be prevented. Children with sexual behavior problems can learn to respect themselves and others. They can learn to demonstrate healthy boundaries and behaviors, even when the reasons for the sexual behavior problems remain unclear.

> "Having a child who acts out sexually with other children can feel very isolating. The group helped me know that other kids have the same problem. I learned that people are willing to help. I am not alone."
>
> —Parent of an 8-year-old boy
>
> "Without support, I would have been a totally depressed person because it is very hard to deal with alone."
>
> —Parent of a 5-year-old girl
>
> "At first, when Devon acted out on my daughter, Cleo, I couldn't separate him from his father, my ex-husband. My anger toward my ex went to my son. I thought Devon would become a pervert or something. Now I realize he is just a boy who saw things he shouldn't have. I know that he can grow up to be a good man. He has learned a lot and made a lot of progress, and so have I."
>
> —Parent of a 10-year-old boy and 5-year-old girl

TWO

Background Information about Sexual Development and Sexual Behavior Problems

Sexual Development

Child-development books and other educational materials for parents rarely include any information about sexual development. Those books also hardly ever explain the difference between typical/normal sexual behavior and sexual behavior problems. Many parents are unsure how to know when a certain sexual behavior—such as when a child touches another child's private parts—might be "playing doctor" or might signify a more serious issue. This chapter will provide information about typical sexual development and how it is different from sexual behavior problems.

Children's sexual awareness starts in infancy and continues to strengthen throughout preschool and school-age years. All aspects of children's development—including cognitive, language, motor, social, emotional, and sexual development—are linked to each other. The table below gives examples of young children's general development and how they learn throughout the preschool years. The relationship between children's general development and their sexual behavior is provided in the second column. For example, young children seek pleasure and avoid discomfort or pain, so if they are uncomfortable in their clothes, they will take them off, not thinking about being nude in front of others. Preschool-age children have little sense of modesty.

Knowing about children's behavior and how it changes as they grow can help caregivers determine if a child's sexual behavior is typical or something to be concerned about.

The following sections provide more details about the development of

Preschool Children's Development and Behavior

Typical Cognitive, Language, and Social Development in Preschool Children	Typical Sexual Development and Behavior
Young children seek pleasure. They do not see themselves from other people's viewpoints. They are not self-conscious.	They often lack modesty and want to be comfortable. They will undress and run around nude in front of others. They may appear to not care about how other people feel because they don't fully understand the impact of their behavior on others.
They are curious about the world, about how things work, and about how things are similar and different from each other.	They are curious about physical differences between boys and girls and between children and adults. This curiosity includes wanting to see how boys' and girls' body parts are different.
They learn through their senses, especially by using sight and touch.	They examine other children's bodies ("I'll show you mine if you show me yours") and discover that touching their own genitals is pleasurable.
They have a rapidly growing vocabulary.	They use words related to urination ("pee-pee") and defecation ("poo-poo") when labeling their private parts. These words can be exciting to children who will use the words repeatedly, particularly with other kids. Young children will use the technical labels (such as vagina, vulva, penis, anus), if taught these terms.
They learn about behaviors by watching the people around them and imitating them.	They imitate behaviors of other children and adults, and play "doctor," "house," or "mommy and daddy" with other children.
Children want to avoid being punished by their parents. They try to avoid discomfort, including getting in trouble. They want approval, praise, and rewards from their parents.	Whether or how often a child repeats sexual behavior is often related to how caregivers respond to the child's initial sexual behavior.
Preschool children have limited ability to plan and control their behavior. They have a poor understanding of the long-term consequences of their behavior.	Children's typical sexual behavior (such as curiously looking at another child) is unplanned. The behavior is impulsive, without much thought.
Children often play make-believe. They often pretend to be something or someone else.	They may play or dress up as people of the opposite sex.

sexual knowledge and behavior in children. At the end of this section, differences between normal sex play and sexual behavior problems are discussed in more detail.

Sexual Development in Early Childhood: Infants, Toddlers, and Preschoolers (Ages 0 to 6)

Sexual Knowledge

Children as young as 3 years of age can identify their own gender (girl or boy), and then, soon after, can identify the gender of others. At first, children judge the differences between the sexes on observable features found in the culture (such as hair length), although by age 3 or 4 years, many children are aware of differences in the bodies of boys and girls.

Young children often have a limited understanding of pregnancy and birth. By age 6, however, they may know that babies grow in their mother's womb and they may know the differences between birth by caesarean section or by vaginal delivery. What children know about adults' sexual behavior and intimacy is influenced by what the children have seen and heard. Preschool children mostly know about such things as kissing and cuddling. About one in five 6-year-olds knows something about more explicit sexual behaviors.

Sexual Behavior

Preschool children are curious in general and tend to actively learn about the world through listening, looking, touching, and imitating. Preschool children express their general curiosity about the world with questions. They also imitate behavior they have seen and they explore their own bodies and others'. Children ages 2 to 5 years old tend to look at others' bodies even when those people are nude. Children that age do not tend to respect physical boundaries, and may stand too close to other people. They often touch their own sexual body parts, even in public. Young children may touch adult women's breasts, particularly their mothers'. Dressing up and pretending to be the opposite sex (such as a boy wearing his sister's dress) is also not unusual throughout this developmental period.

Sexual play (showing one's own sexual body parts and looking at or briefly touching other children's body parts) is not unusual for preschool-age children. Sexual play is discussed in more detail below in the school-age development section. Culture and social context influence how often these typical behaviors occur.

Children as young as 7 months may touch and play with their own private parts. Infants and young children's self-touch behavior appears largely related to curiosity and soothing feeling. From infancy on, children begin to explore the world. They learn about things that feel good and things that don't. Various parts of the human body have a high concentration of nerve endings that make those areas very sensitive to touch. For example, the fingertips, mouth, anus, and genital areas are highly sensitive. Children discover the sensations in these areas during their normal exploratory behavior. Think of self-touch of private parts as a similar activity to when your child sucks her thumb or snuggles with a soft blanket. Even as infants, children are capable of sexual arousal; newborn baby boys can have penile erections. It's an automatic bodily response, just like cutting a fresh onion can make your eyes water (even though you are not sad). These behaviors are very different from adult sexuality and self-stimulatory behavior. With young children, bodily responses don't involve sexual fantasy; they are just something that feels soothing or good.

Sexually explicit, planned, or aggressive sexual acts are *not* a typical part of sexual development. Other rare sexual behaviors include putting objects in the vagina or rectum, putting one's mouth on sexual parts, or pretending toys are having sex.

Sexual Development in School-Age Children (Ages 7 to 12)

Physical Development

Children usually begin puberty during this age period. Puberty is a time in children's lives in which their bodies change in many ways, allowing them to be capable of reproducing (of having children). Puberty is a time that brings many changes in children's bodies, minds, emotions, and relationships with others. It is an important time of life, honored in many cultures through coming-of-age rituals during adolescence. It is also often a difficult time for youths as well as their caregivers.

Puberty usually begins for children around age 10. Some girls may begin to experience changes in their bodies as early as age 7 or 8. For girls, early stages of puberty start with a growth spurt in height, followed by a growth spurt in weight. Boys' growth spurts often take place later than girls'. A boy's puberty begins when his testicals and scrotum begin to grow, his vocal cords get bigger, and his voice deepens. The specific age that a child enters puberty varies, depending on such things as nutrition, family genes, and race. The progression with which a child moves through the stages varies, as well. Such differences in the way children move into and through puberty can impact the social adjustment and behavior of young people. For example, a boy who looks younger than his classmates and has a higher-pitched voice may feel awkward about the fact that he is not like his friends.

Sexual Knowledge

Children's knowledge of pregnancy, birth, and adult sexual activity increases during their elementary-school years. By age 10, most children can have a basic and fairly realistic understanding of puberty, how "babies

are made," pregnancy, and childbirth. The accuracy of their sexual knowledge, however, depends in large part on the children's exposure to correct information and educational material. Since parents often find communicating with their children about bodily changes and sexual matters uncomfortable, children frequently turn to other sources of information. They may learn inaccurate sexual information and troublesome values from other youth and from movies, magazines, song lyrics, the Internet, and television.

Sexual Behavior
By age 7 and 8, children begin to understand the rules of society and apply those rules to a variety of situations. Children this age start to understand that most sexual behaviors are not allowed. Children often become modest during these years, too. Girls, especially, become shy about undressing in front of others. They also become more private about their personal grooming activities (such as bathing). School-age children's sexual behaviors become more shaped by their friends and acquaintances than they were at younger ages. They tend to be hesitant to display any sorts of sexual behaviors when anyone else can see them. Children's sexual

behaviors continue to occur throughout this school-age period, but these behaviors are often hidden from view of others. Caregivers may not even know that such sexual behaviors are taking place.

School-age children are especially interested in the media and are likely to seek out television shows, Internet sites, movies, and pictures in publications that include nudity. Self-touch behaviors occur with increasing frequency in boys during this developmental period. Interest in the opposite sex increases as children approach their teens, and interactive behaviors are initiated with the playful teasing of others. A small but significant number (about 7 to 10 percent) of children are involved in more explicit sexual activity, including sexual intercourse, by the age of 13.

Normal Sexual Play Among Children

Sexual play is different from problematic sexual behaviors. Childhood sexual play (like "playing doctor") includes behaviors that involve private parts and is

- unplanned (that is, happens out of the blue);
- intermittent (that is, happens every once in a while);
- agreed to by both children (neither child objects);
- something that involves children of a similar age, size, and developmental level;
- merely curious in nature;
- an activity that may involve physical touch; and
- not accompanied by anger, fear, or strong anxiety.

In other words, normal child development involves some degree of behavior focused on sexual body parts and curiosity about sexual behavior. Sex play occurs between children of similar ages and abilities, who know and play with each other regularly, rather than between strangers. Since most of the time, boys typically play with boys and girls play with girls, sexual play often occurs between children of the same gender, and it may include siblings.

Researchers have learned a lot about childhood sex play through asking young adults about their own childhood experiences. Some things they learned is that sex play among children

- occurs between children who know and play with each other already, including siblings and children of the same sex;
- is common (many of the adults reported at least one childhood experience);
- may not be discovered by parents;
- is seen as positive or neutral, if the behavior is true sex play (if it involves children of similar ages, and no force or aggression is used) and not between siblings; and
- is not related to whether the child will be heterosexual or gay or lesbian as an adult.

Children who participate in typical childhood sexual play are basically being curious. They don't obsess about sexual activity, or practice more advanced sexual behaviors, such as intercourse or oral sex. Intrusive, planned, forced, or aggressive sexual acts are *not* part of typical or normal sex play of children, but are, instead, problem behaviors.

In the first example of families provided in the introduction of this booklet, the two sons of the Cornelison family were demonstrating sex play. The children's behavior was between two brothers of about the same age. They were not upset or angry. Instead, they were just curious. The behavior was not planned and happened when they were changing clothes. Neither child was pressured to do the behavior, although both were somewhat embarrassed to have been discovered. On the other hand, the sexual behavior of Ryan McFarland in the second example is of more concern due to the four-year age difference between him and his neighbor. The sexual behavior of Jerry Kastner in the last example is particularly concerning as he and his classmates used force with a younger student.

Caregivers' Responses to Sexual Play

In the first example described on pages 9 and 10, Mr. and Mrs. Cornelison's two sons were involved in sex play. After discovering the situation, the Cornelisons asked what they should do, or if they should ignore the behavior because it was just "normal curiosity." Rather than ignoring these behaviors, the best response a caregiver can have is to use the discovery of the sex play as "a teachable moment." The situation can serve as a lesson. When children are involved in sex play, they are primarily being curious. These children benefit from having an adult explain information and the rules about relationships and intimacy to them.

Parents can respond to typical "sex play" or sexual behavior by calmly providing education in the area that appears most relevant to the situation. Responses can include

- education about accurate names and functions of all body parts;
- information about social rules of behavior and privacy;
- information about how to respect their own bodies and those of others;
- information about friendships and intimate relationships; and
- sex education that is appropriate for the child's age and developmental level.

Children will often respond well to accurate information, to the opportunity to have their questions answered, to good supervision, and to reminders of social rules. Books are often useful in this educational process. Suggestions for a few books are provided at the end of this booklet.

Cultural Impact on Sexual Development

Family and community values and beliefs are the foundation of the culture within which children are raised. A child's knowledge of sex and

> "I was sexually abused as a child so I've always been very watchful and sensitive to possible abuse of my own children. Around Halloween, my 4-year-old daughter was found naked with her best friend and they were giggling and pointing to each other's bottoms. They had been changing into their costumes to play. After talking with her friend's mother and the girls, I realize now that they were just being kids and curious. I, and the mother of my daughter's friend, both talked one-on-one with our daughters about private parts and privacy rules. The kids seemed to understand and now they wear leotards when they want to play dress up and change a lot."
>
> —Parent of a 4-year-old girl

the child's sexual behavior are thus shaped by the values and beliefs held by the child's own family and community. A variety of cultural attitudes shape what children understand and respond to. Children's cultural environments affect how they understand body changes, public and private sexual behavior, pregnancy, birth, intimacy, and relationships.

Three examples of cultural differences include the following:

- Communities may follow social or cultural customs/practices when teaching their children about sex education and relationships. For example, discussions on sexual behavior with children may be considered appropriate for some individuals to have (such as, when grandmothers teach granddaughters) but taboo for others (such as, when uncles talk with their nieces).
- Some cultures have specific activities, rituals, or stories involved in the teaching of their youths and in helping with their transition into adulthood.
- Social environments in which nudity is acceptable and physical privacy is not reinforced are related to higher frequencies of typical (nonintrusive) sexual behaviors in the children than are social environments that reinforce modesty and privacy.

Impact of Media on Sexual Development and Sexual Behavior Problems

Children obtain sexual knowledge through many different sources. Both obvious and subtle messages about sexual behavior are provided through family, friends, neighbors, and the community. Messages about sexuality are also provided through a variety of media sources such as television, movies, music videos, music lyrics, video games, magazines, the Internet, and cell-phone communication. Unfortunately, explicit sexual activities are found during "family time" television shows and on cartoon/children's channels, as well.

Exposure to explicit sexual acts through different media sources can have a big impact on a child's behavior. In the second example provided at the beginning of the booklet, Mr. McFarland's son, Ryan, had engaged in humping behavior with his younger neighbor. Mr. McFarland wondered how Ryan could have learned such behavior. One possible answer was that Ryan had observed sexual acts in movies or on television, was curious about these behaviors, and then had attempted to act them out with his friend. Nowadays, caregivers have to be extra careful about monitoring what their children are exposed to through multiple media. Children have many opportunities to observe different

multimedia sources outside of the home. Parents will find it helpful to develop a strong, supportive network of friends who share their values and who can help supervise the children. Caregivers can benefit from educating themselves about the rating systems of games, movies, and shows as well as how to use parental controls available through cable, satellite dish networks, and the Internet.

It is not entirely clear how children sort out the often conflicting messages they receive about sex, affection, and love relationships. Attentive parents who provide close supervision and good communication can help to provide children with the skills to make healthy decisions about their behavior and relationship choices. Even television programs can have a positive impact on youths' sexual knowledge and behavior, particularly when those programs demonstrate actual outcomes (like pregnancies) to sexual behavior and when parents talk with their children about the content of the programs.

Children with Developmental Delays, Disabilities, and Medical Conditions

Both developmental disabilities and medical conditions can impact children's sexual development. For example, children with Down syndrome may start puberty at an early age. Children with Prader-Willi syndrome may start puberty at a later-than-average age. Spinal-cord injuries can cause other types of changes in sexual development. Professionals and family members often are unsure how to understand, accept, and respond to sexual development in individuals with disabilities. As with all children, however, sexual behaviors begin at or around birth, and when children hit puberty, sexual feelings typically strengthen. At that point, many adolescents with developmental disabilities may wish to date or otherwise be in intimate relationships with other youths. Youths with developmental disabilities are less likely to have been provided developmentally appropriate sexual education, due in part to the uncertainty of the adults who are caring for them. Caregivers are encouraged to educate themselves about these issues and to learn how to communicate the information to their youths. Sources of additional information in this area are provided in the resource section in the back of the booklet.

Incidence and Prevalence of Sexual Behavior Problems in Children

No one knows how many children have had sexual behavior problems during their lives. No specific entity or agency is in charge of these youths or tracks their behavior. Sometimes, child protective services are involved with children with sexual behavior problems, especially when the children have been abused or neglected. At times, juvenile or family court could also be involved, especially with older children. Over the last two decades, child protective service systems and juvenile services have had more referrals of children with sexual behavior problems. We don't know if these referrals represent a true increase in the number of children with sexual behavior problems, or if they represent a greater public recognition of and response to the problem, or a combination of both.

THREE

How Do Children Develop Sexual Behavior Problems?

What Causes Sexual Behavior Problems in Children

It is often assumed that all children with sexual behavior problems have been sexually abused. Research indicates, however, that many of those children have no history of sexual abuse. For example, between one-third and one-half of the children with sexual behavior problems that we serve in specialty clinics have had no history of sexual abuse.

A wide range of other factors cause problems in children's sexual behavior, not just sexual abuse. The factors that influence a child's behavior can come from a variety of experiences.

- Some children have seen a lot of violence or have been physically abused.
- Some children have experienced other kinds of traumatic or scary events. They may not know positive, healthy ways to cope. For example, these children may not yet know the words to describe their own feelings and thoughts, and they may act out instead.
- Some children have not experienced any trauma or abuse.
- Some children may act before thinking. Such children may look at or touch other children's private parts without thinking about what they're doing.
- Some children have problems following rules and listening to their parents, teachers, or caregivers

at home, in school, and in the community. These children break a variety of rules, including privacy rules.

- Some children have seen specific sexual acts performed (such as in a movie or music video) and they then act out what they have seen with their friends or siblings.
- Some children have problems making friends their own age. They may instead play with much younger children. They may become curious about sexual behavior when they start puberty and act out with younger children who are their friends and playmates.
- Some children are left on their own to care for themselves, with poorly monitored television and video games as their primary source of entertainment.
- Some children have not had a steady home.
- Some children have parents who struggle to provide close supervision because of a variety of factors, such as depression, substance use, the need to hold multiple jobs, or simply nervousness or insecurity about parenting.

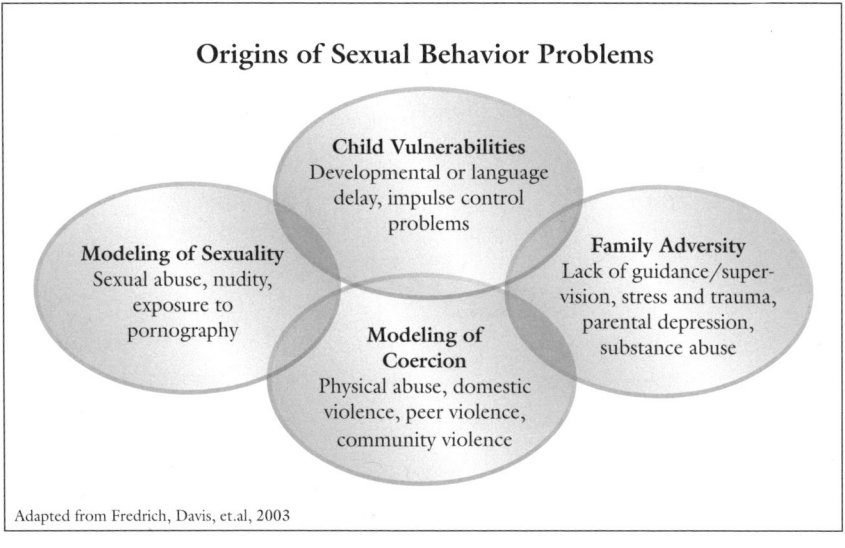

Origins of Sexual Behavior Problems

Child Vulnerabilities
Developmental or language delay, impulse control problems

Modeling of Sexuality
Sexual abuse, nudity, exposure to pornography

Family Adversity
Lack of guidance/supervision, stress and trauma, parental depression, substance abuse

Modeling of Coercion
Physical abuse, domestic violence, peer violence, community violence

Adapted from Fredrich, Davis, et.al, 2003

What If Sexual Abuse is Suspected?

If your child tells someone that another person has touched his or her private parts, or if you suspect sexual abuse, you need to make a referral for an investigation. Some states require that all citizens report any suspected abuse of a child. Ongoing sexual abuse must be stopped to be able to help a child. If you think sexual abuse might have happened, and it has not been previously investigated by Child Protective Services (CPS), then you can report what you suspect so that the appropriate officials can conduct an investigation. Reporting suspected abuse to the authorities can be a scary process for some parents. Parents may be concerned that they will be wrongly accused of abuse themselves. It is critical to stop ongoing abuse if it is occurring, and the first step is to call the authorities. Develop a team approach in working with child protective services, express your desire to protect your child, and make sure the right services are provided. More information about child protective services and legal responses are provided on pages 55–60.

Caregivers or authorities may suspect sexual abuse when children display sexual behavior problems. The investigation at times can indicate that the findings are uncertain, meaning that authorities are not able to confirm that the child has been sexually abused, but they also cannot completely rule it out. Caregivers are understandably concerned about what to do

> "When Alfred acted out sexually with his little sister, I thought he must have been sexually abused. Child Protective Services and the police thoroughly investigated and did not find that he had been abused. Alfred himself has told me no one has touched him. Through the treatment program, I learned that other things impacted Alfred and probably caused that sexual behavior. He has seen some scary things in his life and I suspect he has seen sexual stuff on the TV. The good thing is that now he has learned to make better choices and decisions. And I have learned how to supervise and parent him to help stop it from happening again."
>
> —Parent of an 11-year-old boy and 7-year-old girl

when sexual abuse is suspected. In these situations, we caution caregivers against frequently questioning their child during or after an investigation of possible abuse. Questioning a child repeatedly can actually hinder the investigation process. In addition, it can cause distress and confusion in the child.

If no evidence exists of ongoing sexual abuse or exposure to trauma or sexualized materials, children often can respond to treatment of the sexual behavior problems. Further, with education about child-abuse-prevention skills, children may later reveal details of past sexual abuse, if it had occurred. Abuse-prevention skills help children understand what behaviors are okay and not okay. Those skills teach children that if someone touches their private parts, that person is breaking a rule. Children can also learn which adults to tell when these situations happen. (Abuse-prevention skills are discussed more thoroughly in the treatment section on pages 42–43.) Caregivers are advised to be available to listen, but not to repeatedly question children about possible past sexual abuse.

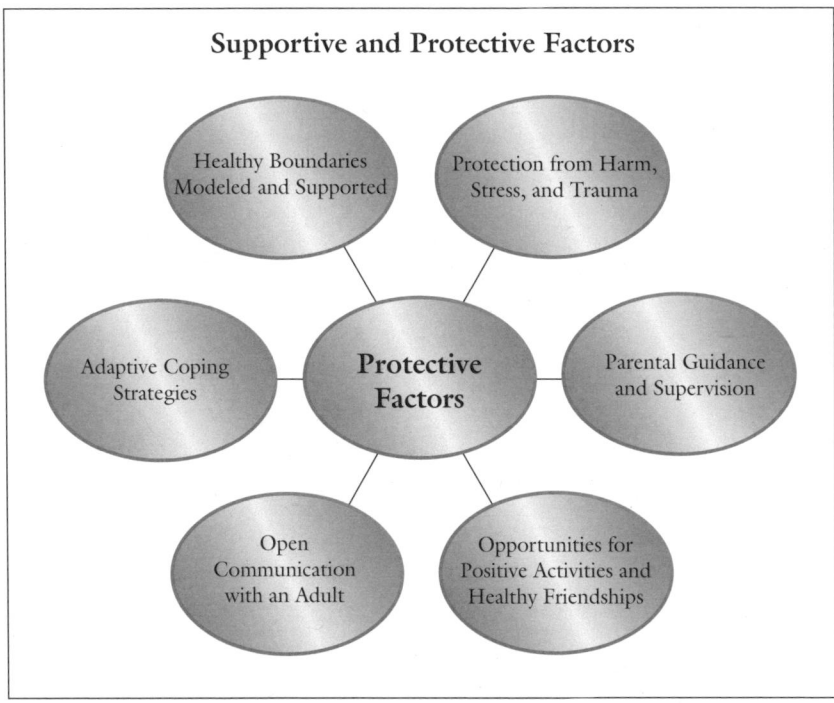

Protective Factors That Prevent the Onset and Continuation of Sexual Behavior Problems

Families and communities have many characteristics that can provide protection for children. Identify those positive factors in your own life and connect with groups that support these messages for your children. Some protective factors include

- the ability of caring, informed adults to be able to talk openly to children about relationships, intimacy, and sexual-education matters;
- close supervision and guidance of children;
- opportunities for children to be involved in age-appropriate activities (for example, sports, boys/girls clubs, after-school activities, and craft activities);
- friends who are caring and who make good decisions;
- warm relationships with caring adults;
- clear, positive messages about modesty, boundaries, and privacy;
- protection for your child from scary or traumatic events, including media coverage of such events as wars, bombings, or shootings; and
- closely observing what your child watches on television and in the movies or is exposed to in music and on the Internet.

Impact of Sexual Behavior Problems on Other Children

Children who have experienced sexual behaviors initiated by other children can have a wide range of responses. Childhood "sexual play" experiences have been viewed as neutral or positive when the children become adults. For example, we would expect that the sons in the Cornelison family in the first example of the introduction will respond well to education provided by their parents. No negative impact would be predicted.

However, when the sexual behavior is problematic (such as coercive or aggressive), the experience can potentially have a detrimental effect on the child. For example, the girl that was held down by Jerry Kastner in the last example may have bad dreams or other symptoms after that experience. The negative effects may be similar to those experienced during sexual abuse by adolescents or adults. Factors that make a difference in how big an impact such sexual behavior might have include

- the length of time in which the behaviors take place (sexual behaviors that occur over a longer period of time are more problematic);
- how many times the behaviors happened;
- the type and closeness of the relationship among the children (such as whether they were siblings, close friends, acquaintances, or strangers);
- use of aggression or force;
- the child's recent functioning (children who were doing poorly before the sexual behaviors are more likely to be negatively impacted); and
- the response and support by the caregivers.

Children's responses to these behaviors differ. Some children have almost no reaction or trauma symptoms. Others may experience things like nightmares and fears, may startle easily to loud noises or sudden movements, or may try to avoid anything that reminds them of the event. Still others develop symptoms of depression, anxiety (such as difficulty in separating from parents), behavior problems, social and peer problems, or even sexual behaviors themselves.

FOUR

Taking Action: Safety Planning for Children with Sexual Behavior Problems

After parents determine that their child has indeed demonstrated sexual behavior problems, parents may have a variety of reactions and responses toward the child. It can be helpful for parents to find ways to become calm and provide support. Remember that with close supervision and appropriate treatment, children can get back on a positive path.

In many communities, therapy or other interventions may not be able to start immediately, but caregivers can start doing many things immediately to help prevent future sexual behavior problems.

1. **Close supervision is important when the child is with other children.** Children who have acted out sexually with other children need continuous visual supervision. Visual supervision means that you can see your child at all times when the child is with other children. Continuous visual supervision is difficult to maintain, however, so families often have to work closely with support systems (such as relatives, friends, and neighbors) to create such oversight. It is important that the supervision be done without fail to insure the safety of other children and to prevent the behavior from becoming a habit.
2. **The child with sexual behavior problems should not sleep in the same bed with other children.** We also advise that the child sleep in a room alone. Some families are not able to accomplish this arrangement, however, for financial or cultural reasons. Other ways to

maintain appropriate monitoring may need to be put in place, such as *not* having your child with sexual behavior problems share a bedroom with younger children, having audio or video monitors, or having other safety measures in place. If your child has nightmares or sleeping problems, he or she can be comforted and put back in his/her own bed or allowed to sleep in your room in a sleeping bag on the floor (this applies particularly to younger children).

3. **Communicate clear rules and expectations about privacy and appropriate sexual behavior to all your family members**. It is important that all members of the family know and observe these rules. All children and adults in the home should be included in a discussion of the privacy rules. Examples of Private Parts Rules and/or Sexual Behavior Rules are provided on page 27.

4. **Have privacy rules in place**. Caregivers should insist on privacy in the bedrooms and bathrooms. Families need to have clear rules in place about entering bedrooms (such as always knocking before entering). Parents can take steps (such as locking the door) to make sure that children cannot simply walk in and observe adult sexual activity.

5. **Personal self-care should occur in private**. Once a child has demonstrated a sexual behavior problem with other children, the child needs to bathe alone and should take care of personal self-care in the bathroom without the presence of other children. If the child is young enough to need help with washing, bathing, or using the bathroom, a parent or another appropriate adult should provide assistance.

6. **An adult should remain in charge of all the children**. Children with sexual behavior problems should not be given any opportunities for assuming a role of authority over other children. This means that the child who

has had sexual behavior problems should not babysit or be told to "watch" other children while a parent cooks dinner, runs a quick errand, etc.

7. **Children need to be protected from sexually explicit media.** Sexually explicit materials, such as what is found in some magazines, videos, computer files, shopping catalogues, and television programs, should not be available to the children in the home. Children need to be supervised closely while they are on the computer to make sure that they are viewing appropriate material. Safety measures need to be in place for cable, satellite dish networks, and the Internet.

8. **Parents and other adults should demonstrate modesty in the child's presence**. There should be no nudity, partial nudity, or explicit displays of sexual behavior by parents or other adults or teenagers in front of the child. It has become fashionable for some people in public to show underwear, bras, the upper section of the buttocks, and other private parts areas. These types of fashions are not recommended for families with children who have had sexual behavior problems. It is appropriate, however, for adults to show affection (such as holding hands, kissing, and hugging) to each other and the children.

Private Parts Rules and Sexual Behavior Rules

Throughout childhood, children learn safety rules. For example:

- Don't touch hot stoves.
- Don't run into the street.
- Wear a safety helmet when you are on your bicycle.

Children with sexual behavior problems often do not have a clear understanding of safety rules about their own bodies. They do not understand the need to respect themselves and other people. It is important for all children, especially those with sexual behavior problems, to learn to follow safety and privacy rules, such as the Private Parts Rules or the Sexual Behavior Rules. The simple rules below can be integrated in your family's safety rules.

Private Parts Rules or Privacy Rules (For Preschool-Age Children)

1. No touching other people's private parts. (This includes kicking, hitting, biting, hurting, etc.)
2. No other people can touch your private parts. (The person doing the touching would be the one breaking the rule. Exceptions to this rule are for caregivers who may need to help with hygiene and for doctors who may need to check to make sure that all parts of a child's body are healthy.)
3. No showing of private parts to other people. (Or: Keep your clothes on when other people can see you.)
4. No touching of private parts in public. (Or: Touching your own private parts when you are alone is OK.)

Sexual Behavior Rules (For School-Age Children)

1. It is not OK to show your private parts to other people.
2. It is not OK to look at other people's private parts.
3. It is not OK to touch other people's private parts.
4. It is OK to touch your private parts as long as it is in private and does not take too much time.
5. It is not OK to use sexual language or make other people uncomfortable with your sexual behavior.

Additional information for caregivers about applying these rules to their family is provided on pages 30–32.

Caregivers are often uncomfortable about teaching accurate labels for private parts. We have heard a variety of labels in our clinics, in addition to

> "Learning the Private Parts Rules was very helpful. The rules helped him understand what is acceptable and what is not. Also he knows who to go to if someone tries to break the rules with him."
>
> —Parent of a 6-year-old boy

"pee-pee" and "poo-poo," such as "cookie jar," "chicken," or "peanuts." We recommend that all children learn the correct names for body parts, including private parts. Some of the reasons to teach the specific names, such as penis, vulva, vagina, breasts, and buttocks, are as follows:

- It is easier for children to report when someone has tried to touch their private parts if they know the correct words.
- It gives the message that these are just parts of a child's body, rather than something that is problematic.
- It gives the message that body parts can be talked about directly with the caregivers, rather than being something hidden or vague (such as "down there").
- Other names for private parts can be confusing for the children.
- Children can give more specific descriptions when they tell an adult about a physical problem (such as pain, itching, or other physical problems).

For children who are multicultural, caregivers may wish to use labels from languages other than English. For example, members of some American Indian tribes may prefer to use their tribal language when teaching about body parts.

It is important for a child to be able to describe what happened when he or she has been sexually abused. When children do not have accurate words for body parts, they are often unable to provide important details needed to protect them from the impacts of the abuse. Too often, young children can only report vague information, such as, "He hurt me down there," and child protective services and law enforcement are unable to

> "One day while waiting in the checkout line at the grocery store, my 4-year-old son bumped into the basket and then started singing, 'I hit my penis! I hit my penis!' At first, I was mortified. But then I realized, it's just part of his body, and I'm glad he knows the name, in case anything should ever happen to him. I looked at the checkout clerk and other customers, and they smiled knowingly—young active boys are just that way. Afterwards, I talked with my son about public and private language."
>
> —Parent of a 4-year-old boy

accurately determine what happened. Help your children to become knowledgeable by teaching them accurate information about their bodies in age-appropriate terms. Help them to learn which adults they can talk to when they have questions or concerns about private matters.

There can be downsides to teaching young and especially impulsive children the correct terms for private parts, because sometimes these children will use the terms in public. Teaching children public and private language as well as public and private behavior can help. The reasons for teaching the correct names, however, outweigh a little public embarrassment if your child talks about or asks about private parts in public.

Young children will benefit from information that they can see or touch. We have found it helpful for children to understand the general term "private parts" and to learn that these are the parts of our body that we keep covered when around other people, even when we are swimming. Our bathing suits cover our private parts.

> "It has helped Maria to learn more about her private parts, and why she should not show them or see others."
>
> —Parent of a 6-year-old girl
>
> "Learning the Sexual Behavior Rules helped him to realize rules of proper behavior in a manner any child can understand."
>
> —Parent of a 10-year-old boy

Pictures of children in bathing suits such as this one can help your child to visualize where his or her private parts are.

Here are some of the things you can do to help prevent future sexual behavior problems, by using Private Parts Rules or Sexual Behavior Rules:

1. Develop specific rules for your family, worded in a manner that you are comfortable with. Name the rules something that you can refer to in public, to help remind your children to follow the rules, such as the Bathing Suit Rules, or Privacy Rules.

2. Rehearse the rules at home to help your child understand that these rules apply to home life as well as to group situations. Many rules in your children's lives will differ, depending on where they are (for example, rules at the park are different from rules at Grandma's house, which are different from rules at home). Your children need to learn that Private Parts Rules are always in place, no matter where they are.
3. Have a regular "family time" at home in which your family checks in about how things are going in general and ends with a fun activity. At these family times, periodically check to see if your children are able to recall the Private Parts Rules.
4. Praise your children for their positive behavior. When they are being good, let them know what they are doing well. For example, if your daughter has been getting into the physical space of her siblings (such as constantly wanting to hug and kiss them), praise her when she plays well with her siblings and leaves respectful spaces between their bodies.
5. Have an agreed-upon gesture or word that you can use when your children look like they are about to violate a Private Parts Rule. This approach is most useful for behaviors that are frequent. A caregiver may use a hand signal (such as pointing up) or a verbal cue (such as saying, "Remember the Bathing Suit Rule"). The cue should be decided with children before a caregiver uses it so that the children know what the cue means.
6. If your children come to talk with you before breaking a Private Parts Rule, praise them. Encourage them to talk with you any time they are struggling with the rules. Decide together what each child will do to obey the Private Parts Rules.
7. Encourage activities that make breaking Private Parts Rules unlikely for your children during times when they are most likely to act out. These activities can be

- ones that use energy, such as bike riding, running, or playing catch (avoid body-contact activities, such as wrestling, tickling, or roughhousing);
- ones that take concentration and that will distract your child (non-violent video games are sometimes good, as well as the game "Concentration," or board games); and
- ones that provides appropriate physical nurturing, like holding hands, stroking your child's hair, or patting your child's back (this kind of caring touch can help fill a need for physical contact in appropriate ways).

8. Use redirection, reminders, and distraction. For example, if your child looks like he might make a poor decision, redirect him to something he should be doing instead.
9. Let your child know what the consequences will be for breaking the Private Parts Rules. Not every behavior needs a time-out. Make the consequences relate logically to your child's behavior, if possible. For example, if you catch your child watching an "R" rated movie on television, the consequence could be that he cannot watch television for the next couple of days.
10. Ask for support from others in your child's life (daycare workers, babysitters, friends, teachers, and relatives) to reinforce the Private Parts Rules.

"My 7-year-old son was playing with his same-age cousin. I heard him say, 'Let's play boyfriend and girlfriend.' I knew that this could lead to a big problem. I grabbed some puppets, put them on my hands, jumped behind a chair, and started acting out a puppet show. They got so excited they wanted to make up their own puppet shows, and they played with the puppets for the next hour! Distraction really worked!"

—PARENT OF A 7-YEAR-OLD BOY

Respecting Other People's Space: Teaching Good Boundaries

Children with sexual behavior problems often have trouble knowing when they have moved too closely into another person's space or physical boundary. Getting into other people's personal space causes them problems with other kids and with others at school and at home. For example, these children may not be able to keep their hands to themselves, and may always have to be touching the people around them. Or they may be the kind of children who run up and give a big hug and kiss to a stranger they just met, such as Summer in the third example in the introduction. Not only is this behavior disrespectful of the other person, but it is also risky, because such children may be more vulnerable to being targeted by adults with intentions to harm them.

Another way children with sexual behavior problems may have difficulties with boundaries is in protecting their own personal spaces. They may not be assertive when other people are too close to them.

Thus, it is important for children to learn to respect other people's physical boundaries and to protect their own. Such knowledge is especially important for children with a history of sexual behavior problems. The idea of "boundaries" is fairly difficult for young children to grasp. One method that makes it possible for a young child to visualize his or her "space" is to use a hula hoop. (If you use a hula hoop to teach boundaries, though, first allow your child to play with it, or the child will have difficulty paying attention.) If you do not have a hula hoop, demonstrate "space" by holding out your arms level with the ground.

- Have your child sit in the middle of the hula hoop.
- Explain that all people have "space" around them, and that they have the right to say who can be in the space and who can't.
- Explain that when someone else enters that space without permission, the person inside the space often feels uncomfortable.
- Give your children words to use to ask before going into someone else's hula space, such as, "May I give you a hug?" or "May I sit here?"

- Give children assertive (not too aggressive or too passive) words to use to tell other people to step out of their hula space, such as, "Please move over."
- Teach children ways to greet people that do not involve hugging or sitting in their laps, such as holding out their hand and shaking hands. Such greetings can be made more personal for special people, by using something like a high five.

Individuals in families, churches, and other cultural and community groups have their own greeting rituals and areas of comfort regarding physical space. Some groups remain at arm's length when their members get together, while people in other groups stand right next to each other when talking, even though the people might have just met. Some church communities greet members with a hug and kiss on the cheek. There is no "right" response to managing these different community rules for *all* children with sexual behavior problems. With professional support, you can develop rules and teaching strategies that fit your own children. Older children often can learn different greeting rituals for different groups of people, whereas younger children or impulsive children may not understand why they can hug some people they know but not others.

Children need to know how to respond when they feel someone has gotten too close to them. Further, they should be taught to respect others' wishes for greater physical space.

Guidelines to Follow If You Find Your Child Engaged in Sexual Behavior

By using the guidelines and rules above, and by keeping close visual supervision of your child, most sexual behavior problems can be prevented. If supervision becomes lax or if for some other reasons your child displays an inappropriate sexual behavior, the following list provides some guidelines for responses.

1. Try to remain calm and keep an even volume and tone of voice. Count to ten, take deep breaths, or use other strategies to help calm down. When you remain calm, it helps you to have better responses than when you react with strong emotions. When you remain calm, it helps your child to understand that it's the behavior you don't approve of, not the child.
2. If needed, have the children get dressed and go to separate areas of the home.
3. After you have all the children dressed and in a safe place, check your level of emotions again. If you are in control and at least somewhat calm, proceed with the steps listed below. If you continue to be very upset, find some outside source of support, such as a professional, a partner, or a friend. Continue to take deep breaths.
4. Once calm, evaluate the situation. Ask the children individually what happened. Keep the questions open ended so that they can tell you in their own words (rather than just by answering yes or no). Ask things like: What happened? Who thought of doing this? How did you learn about this?
5. Try to determine how problematic the behaviors were, using the information in the first chapter, "Definitions and Responses."
6. If your child, who initiated the behavior, has been taught privacy rules, remind your child of the specific Private Parts Rule that he or she is breaking (for example, "Remember, no touching others' private parts").
7. If a consequence is necessary, provide it immediately in a firm, but calm manner, such as, "Because you tried to touch Tommy's private parts, Tommy has to go home, and you can't play with him for the rest of the week."
8. After the consequence, help your child to think of things that he or she could have done instead of the sexual behavior, such as talking to an adult, playing with a toy, or drawing a picture.

9. Let your child know that you believe in his ability for self-control. Emphasize that he can try something different next time. "Next time you think about touching Susie's private parts, you can play _____ instead, or you can come ask me for help." Give your child the words to say and practice them with him.
10. Determine if consequences are not necessary and redirect your child to another activity. If the behavior is okay when done in private (such as when a child touches herself), redirect her to her bedroom or to another nonpublic place.
11. Talk with the caregivers of the other children involved, if appropriate.
12. Praise your child during times when he or she displays positive behaviors.
13. Remember that children with sexual behavior problems always need close visual supervision when with other children.

Developing a Support Team: Communicating with Other Adults

Raising a child who has had sexual behavior problems can bring great stress paired with a sense of isolation to the caregivers. Children's sexual behavior is a hard topic to talk about with other adults. It is important for you to have at least one other adult that you can talk to in private about your child's sexual behavior and about your thoughts, feelings, fears, beliefs, and other related topics. Children are cared for by multiple adults (including teachers, parents of the children's friends, neighbors, and relatives). These adults will need to know the appropriate level of supervision to provide. But no single rule can be applied to all children who have had a sexual behavior problem. Decisions about who should be included in the support team must be made individually, and often with assistance of trained professionals.

A wider net of support is needed for children who

- have had frequent or impulsive sexual behavior problems in a variety of settings (such as at home and at daycare), because they will need closer visual supervision;
- have poor decision-making skills and combative behavior;
- have demonstrated aggressive or demanding behavior; or
- have significant developmental issues.

While it is important for you to have other supportive adults with whom to discuss the details of these situations, it is not necessary for all adults in your child's life to know about the behavior. In fact, in some cases, it may be harmful for certain adults to know the details of your child's past trauma experiences and sexual behaviors, especially if those adults use the information to label and make fun of the child. Typically, the information that needs to be shared with other adults is that

- your child has a history of making poor decisions when unsupervised with other children. At times it also can be helpful to tell those other adults that things have happened in the past to the child, which have interfered with his/her ability to make good decisions with other children (such as abuse);
- visual supervision is needed to make sure all children are safe;
- a plan is needed to prevent potentially risky situations, such as when your child goes to the bathroom with other children without an adult to supervise; and
- other safeguards may be needed in situations that typically have lower levels of supervision (such as playing on the playground).

Potentially Risky Situations

Over the years, we have found some situations more risky for a child who might be inclined to break a Private Parts Rule again. By being aware of these potentially risky situations, you can better plan to avoid them or to incorporate safeguards and supervision to prevent future sexual behavior problems. High-risk situations include the following:

- Sleepovers
- Contact sports, such as wrestling
- Holiday times
- Summer vacations (which are less structured than school environments)
- Camping out
- Recess, when poorly supervised
- Summer camps
- Shared bathrooms at school, etc.
- Cell-phone use
- Unstructured, poorly supervised activities
- Poorly supervised Internet, video game, or cable use

The level of supervision and information provided to the supervising adults will differ depending on the needs of your child. Typically, until your child with sexual behavior problems has a long period of demonstrating good boundaries and decision making, without breaking the Sexual Behavior Rules (over a period of time like three months), the risky situations noted above should be avoided. If situations cannot be avoided while the children are continuing to demonstrate sexual behavior problems, maintain 100 percent visual supervision when your child is with other children.

FIVE

Taking Action: Finding the Right Treatment for Children with Sexual Behavior Problems and Their Families

One of the most important supports for you, if your child has a sexual behavior problem, is to have quality behavioral health treatments. Effective treatments do exist. When a child and his family can get this kind of treatment, it makes a big difference for all involved. The treatments can have positive results for a very long time.

Consult a qualified treatment professional when

- your child demonstrates a sexual behavior problem as described earlier;
- you are uncertain if the behavior was just "playing doctor" or was a sexual behavior problem;
- any child is distressed about the sexual behaviors of another child; or
- you have other serious questions and concerns about your child.

The first steps of the behavioral health provider (therapist) should be to evaluate and assess the situation with your child and your family. This evaluation will help the provider determine if the behavior was a sexual behavior problem, what other concerns or issues might need to be addressed, and what supports and protective factors are present in the family and community.

The evaluation will most likely involve an interview with you and your child (particularly if your child is 7 years old, or older). You and maybe your child's teachers and your child, too, will have to complete an information checklist. Some other tests may have to be given to your child. If Child Protective Services or law enforcement is involved in the case, a summary of their findings will be helpful to the professionals. The professionals will often choose to postpone this evaluation until the completion of the investigation, to prevent any interference with the process.

What Makes a Treatment Program Successful?

Different types of therapies for sexual behavior problems in children have been evaluated by researchers to determine just how effective each one is. Some of the research has examined therapy designed to help sexually abused children, with a goal of reducing the children's sexual behavior problems. Other research has looked at treatments set up to focus specifically on sexual behavior problems. Looking at all the research to date, we have learned about what types of treatment are helpful for children with sexual behavior problems and their families. The main characteristics of effective therapy include

- outpatient treatment (where the child stays in the home and community);
- active and full participation in the treatment by parents and caregivers;
- short-term treatment of approximately three to six months. Short-term treatment is possible if the family attends sessions regularly, actively participates in available services, and practices skills between sessions; and
- Education for caregivers about how to:
  - apply rules about sexual behaviors;
  - improve the quality of their relationship with their children;
  - use parenting strategies that prevent and reduce behavior problems in general;

- address sexual education topics with their children; and
- support abuse-prevention strategies and skills.

Other treatment characteristics that may be helpful include addressing the following topics with the children in age-appropriate ways:

- Privacy rules, sexual behavior rules, and boundary rules
- Abuse-prevention skills
- The labeling and expressing of feelings and skills to reduce distress
- Impulse-control strategies and decision-making skills
- Social skills
- Apologizing and extending empathy toward victims, when children are old enough to understand the value of such caring acts

These treatments have been found to be effective with children who have a wide range of sexual behavior problems, including the types of sexual behavior problems of the children in the examples provided in the

> "The concrete techniques taught gave my daughters some new skills that will be useful in many situations. It reminded me to use praise more and to approach each situation with a calm attitude."
>
> —Parent of 10- and 8-year-old girls
>
> "I am more relaxed now. I do not yell and holler at every little thing they do. I rate the importance of the bad behavior and deal with it accordingly."
>
> —Parent of three boys, ages 7 to 12 years old
>
> "I now treat Houston like a 12-year-old child, instead of expecting him to always know the 'right' thing to do."
>
> —Parent of a 12-year-old boy

> "Both children benefited from learning alongside other children. The key areas of hula space, bubble breaths, and turtle technique became solid, basic family axioms. The children possess confidence and comfort in knowing what the rest of the group knows. This confidence and education has helped my children to understand and act appropriately."
>
> —Parents of a 6-year-old boy and 5-year-old girl
>
> "Johnny now is better at controlling himself and his sexual behavior. He is more comfortable with talking about and telling the truth."
>
> —Parent of an 11-year-old boy

introduction. Even kids who demonstrated aggressive sexual behaviors like Jerry Kastner have responded well to intervention.

Treatment for children with sexual behavior problems is *very different* from treatments for adult sexual offenders. You should avoid treatment programs that are based on adult sexual offender models, such as ones that appear punitive in nature or that focus on sexual arousal or the teaching of arousal reconditioning.

Teaching children Privacy or Sexual Behavior Rules is described on page 27. Strategies to teach abuse-prevention skills and impulse-control skills are described on pages 42–43 and 43–45, respectively.

Abuse-Prevention Skills

Adults who teach and take care of children are responsible for protecting all children from abuse. While most adults feel capable of watching out for strangers who might try to harm children, the reality is that most children are sexually abused by someone they know.

Children with sexual behavior problems are often considered more vulnerable to future sexual abuse victimization than other children. An important goal of treatment is to help you be able to recognize potentially risky behaviors and situations and have the skills to respond effectively.

> "You should always have some trusted adult who will believe you. Never let any adult touch your private parts if they don't have a good reason."
> —12-YEAR-OLD GIRL

The Stop It Now! organization has developed several useful pamphlets that address the prevention of child sexual abuse. The pamphlets, designed specifically for caregivers, can be found at www.stopitnow.org. The recommendations provided by Stop It Now! also support other parenting advice for children with sexual behavior problems. The pamphlets describe how to provide close supervision, monitor media and technology, have good physical boundaries, and address inappropriate talk and behavior. They also suggest that you have an open communication with your children about private parts, rules regarding sexual behaviors, relationships, and intimacy.

Teaching your child the Private Parts Rules or Sexual Behavior Rules allows him or her to learn information about appropriate and inappropriate touch. This information is an important foundation for your child because it teaches the child how to know when someone else is breaking a rule or when activities might hold the potential for abuse. Teaching your child how to respond if someone else attempts to break one of the Private Parts Rules provides abuse-prevention education. Strategies to include in this teaching process are how to get out of a dangerous situation and how to find and talk to an adult. At times the first adult a child tells may not understand or respond, so also teach your child to keep on telling, until someone believes and protects him or her. Teaching your child to tell an adult, even when the child has been told to keep the incident a secret, is important.

Impulse-Control Skills and Decision-Making Skills

Children can be taught helpful strategies to express their feelings, remain in control of their bodies, and follow home and school rules. Preschool children are impulsive by nature, but they can begin to learn to stop and think before acting. Older children with sexual behavior problems may also be impulsive. Something we call the STOP strategy can be taught to your child as a way to remain in control and to appropriately express anger and other feelings. The STOP method includes the following steps, which can be used when children have strong feelings or are about to do something that will get them in trouble:

Stop! relax, and calm down.
Think about what you should do.
Observe and explore choices for responses.
Plan your response.

First, children need to be taught how to recognize feelings and how to know when those feelings are especially intense or strong (such as very angry or scared). Once children recognize a strong feeling, before they say or do anything, they can tell themselves to stop and then can practice calming down. After they are calm, they can think better about what they should do in the situation. You can help your children practice these skills.

For younger children, it can be helpful to give them a story with animal characters to help them visualize the steps. One metaphor that has been

---

"After we learned the STOP method, instead of jumping angrily at the kids, I began using the STOP myself, which helped me deal with the situation."

—PARENT OF TWO GIRLS, AGES 8 AND 11 YEARS OLD

"When he seems like he is going to 'blow,' I now catch him and tell him to, 'Stop, relax, and think.'"

—PARENT OF A 9-YEAR-OLD BOY

"I now tell my son each day to do the *next* right thing. If he can just stop and think about what is the next right thing to do in this very situation, he will stay on the right path."

—PARENT OF AN 11-YEAR-OLD BOY

useful is the image of a turtle that always carries a shell on his back to keep himself safe. You can use a story about turtles, with a wise old turtle who teaches the younger turtles to use their shells when they are feeling strong feelings or are about to get into trouble. The turtles can stop, go into their shell, take deep breaths to calm down, think about what they should do, and go do it! Puppets can help keep the children engaged in learning these steps.

You also can model this strategy for your children. If you are a little frustrated, you can say out loud, "I am beginning to feel frustrated. I need to calm down. I am going to take some deep breaths and count to 10. Then I will make a good decision." Then you can do something that is constructive. You can also gently remind your child to use the STOP method or the turtle method.

We have taught hundreds of families these strategies. We find that not only do the children benefit from learning the strategies, but the parents do, too. Parents report that their children often remind them to use the STOP method, particularly when in the car during heavy traffic.

Apology and Empathy

Parents often comment about being concerned that their child may be a "psychopath," because their child is not demonstrating strong remorse associated with various sexual behavior problems. This is the case with Ms. Blackwood in the third story in the beginning of this booklet. Instead of having this worry, we want to assure you that children are naturally and normally self-focused. Young children do not readily understand and experience other people's perspectives about situations and emotions. Young children follow rules to avoid punishment and receive benefits (rather than for the more altruistic reasons that adults may have).

Of the hundreds of children we have served in our specialty clinic for children with sexual behavior problems, it has been rare that we have had any real concerns that a child was unable to be sensitive to others. More common, and of greater concern to us, are situations in which children have developed a strong sense of shame. In those situations, the children believe that they are worthless, damaged, or bad human beings.

While it is important for children to recognize that breaking the sexual behavior rule is a serious problem, they also need to recognize that they are valuable people who can learn how to follow the rules. A sense of guilt (such as, "I did something I should not have done, and I need to not do it again") is healthy, but shame (such as, "I'm a horrible person who can never do any good") is harmful. Caregivers need to provide and work with the other people in the child's life to communicate the message that the child is loved and loveable; it's the behavior and choice that was not acceptable.

Some therapies for children with sexual behavior problems may include the writing of a mock apology letter to the person with whom the child broke the sexual behavior rule. This letter is for therapeutic purposes only, and is not to be taken home or given to the other child. The letter helps the child to acknowledge that he or she has broken a specific rule, as well

---

Dear Sister,
I am writing because I broke a sexual behavior rule. What I did was not okay because it is dangerous. You might hurt somebody really bad. When I think about what happened, I feel sad, scared, and embarrassed. I have learned some ways to control my behavior. They are the sexual behavior rules and the STOP method. I have been helping myself to not be so sad. If you ever feel uncomfortable around me, you could talk to someone.
Sincerely, Leslie

Dear Leslie,
We want you to know how very proud of you we are. We know that there is so much that has happened and there have been a lot of changes that have taken place. We really feel that you are being strong and we are very proud of you. We appreciate that you listen and do what is asked. We have been pleased that you have opened up a little more each day and that you are talking about your feelings. We know things take time to feel more comfortable and natural, but you are putting in a really good effort. Thank you for your positive attitude. Always know that we will be here for you and loving you. You are very special and important.
Mom and Dad

as to acknowledge the impact that that behavior has had on others. It also describes what the child has learned to be better able to follow the rules, and says what other people can do to stay safe. To provide support to a child through this process, we also ask the caregiver to write a supportive letter to the child about his or her progress.

Trauma Symptoms in Children with Sexual Behavior Problems

Some children with sexual behavior problems have themselves been the victims of something deeply shocking or upsetting. Those children have sometimes been sexually abused, physically abused, or have witnessed violence. They have trauma symptoms, such as nightmares, separation anxiety, the inability to stop thinking about the trauma, or avoidance of things that remind them of the trauma. Both sexual behavior problems and trauma symptoms can be effectively treated with Trauma-Focused Cognitive Behavioral Therapy. This treatment is similar to the one described above, in that it is often done on an outpatient basis with both the caregivers and the child, it is relatively short-term, and it teaches participants information and coping skills. Trauma-Focused Cognitive Behavioral Therapy also provides education about the effects of traumatic events and addresses negative thinking that the child and parents may have. It encourages children to tell what happened in a way that reduces the trauma symptoms around the event (this is called the "trauma narrative"). More information about Trauma-Focused Cognitive Behavioral Therapy can be found at www.nctsnet.org/nctsn_assets/pdfs/promising_practices/TF-CBT_fact_sheet_2-11-05.pdf. Parents can also go to www.nctsnet.org and click on For Parents and Caregivers.

General Behavior Problems in Children with Sexual Behavior Problems

Often, but not always, children with sexual behavior problems have difficulty following rules in general and listening to their caregivers and other adults. They may have Attention Deficit Hyperactivity Disorder (ADHD) and as a result may be impulsive and active. Children with ADHD have difficulty sitting still and listening. They may talk in class, and have difficulties either sitting in their chairs or following the rules at home and at school.

Sometimes children with sexual behavior problems are more resistant, angry, or negative in general. They may yell a lot, argue, and get into fights. They may not listen to their parents or teachers without a good or clear reason. Parents' and teachers' efforts to have the children listen and follow rules just don't seem to work with children who have a long pattern of being combative or argumentative. These children may be diagnosed with Oppositional Defiant Disorder or Conduct Disorder, such as Jerry in the fourth example in the introduction.

These types of behaviors—being impulsive, breaking serious rules, or displaying high levels of activity, anger, or resistance—come out in different amounts of force and strength. In the milder stages, your family may benefit from using different parenting strategies. In this approach, you examine your parenting approaches and seek advice and support to strengthen and implement those strategies. Parenting strategies that can be helpful are as follows:

- Schedule regular positive playtime with your child. This does not have to last long. Even five minutes a day can go a long way. Children strongly desire parents' attention and love. Providing this attention on a regular basis makes a difference.
- Provide consistency in your child's daily routine. Routine activities like waking, breakfast time, after-school time, dinner time, and bath/bedtime are better when they occur at about the same time each day.
- Offer regular recognition of the positive behaviors your child is doing, through praise, stickers, and other methods of acknowledging progress. If you have difficulty thinking of any positive behaviors, then refer to the recommendations under the more extreme side of the continuum.
- Give clear, concise messages. When you need to tell your child to do something, tell your child in a

nice manner and explain the reasons why first. Use messages like, "Marques, we are leaving the house in five minutes. Please put on your shoes."

- ◆ If your child does what you tell him, offer praise!
- ◆ If your child does not follow your request, give your child one warning (Don't repeat a warning a million times). Then, if your child still does not comply, give a consequence (such as a time out). Consistency is *key*. When you become consistent, then your child will learn that he can't get away with the behavior and he will begin to follow rules more consistently.
- Have clear, consistently applied rules. Develop some specific, clear rules for the whole family that everyone must follow. Recognize times when family members do follow the rules. Provide a specific consequence every time a rule is broken.
- Provide opportunities for children to appropriately identify and express their feelings and to apply strategies to remain calm and make good decisions. More details about these strategies are in the section on the treatment of sexual behavior problems.
- STAY CALM. Deep breaths are important.

The parenting strategies listed above are important even with children who have an abuse history. We have often worked with parents whose children have been sexually abused. When children have been abused,

> "I learned to say, 'You are being disrespectful to me, and I want you to stop it now.' I also learned to not yell, and to tell them what to do nicely. Most of all, I've learned to pay more attention to them when they are doing the right thing."
>
> —PARENT OF A 10-YEAR-OLD BOY, AND 8- AND 6-YEAR-OLD GIRLS

their caregivers often have a hard time requiring rules or consequences of the children, because they feel the children have been hurt enough already. This was the case in the example of Ms. Blackwood at the beginning of the booklet. Her granddaughter, Summer, had been sexually abused and Ms. Blackwood was worried that firm rules could upset Summer even more. Summer had been through a difficult time, and Ms. Blackwood wanted her to be happy. It is understandable that a parent will feel that way. Children will often cry and get upset when someone imposes consequences. But you can tell yourself that you are being a good parent if, through a structured and positive environment, you teach your child to make good decisions and follow rules. Treatments found especially helpful for sexually and physically abused children include the teaching of parenting strategies such as the ones above.

If you have told your child to do something, and she becomes upset, causing you to wonder if you are doing something harmful to her, ask yourself:

- Is what I'm asking my child to do reasonable? Are most children her age capable of following this task?
- Is my child choosing not to do what I say? That is, has she heard and understood the instruction and is she capable of doing it, yet is *still* not completing the task?
- Is the consequence I have chosen reasonable (does it "fit the crime")? That is, is the consequence appropriate, given what she is still choosing not to do?

If you can answer yes to all of the above, then know that you are being a good caregiver by *giving* your child this consequence. You are teaching your child the importance of listening to you and following your instructions. You are teaching your child to respect others and to learn self-control.

For children with the most difficult attention problems—impulsiveness, hostility, or poor conduct—professional support is a must. What can help is a treatment called Behavioral Parent Training, which can be provided by a psychologist, social worker, or other licensed mental-health specialist. This treatment teaches you parenting strategies proven effective with children who are combative or impulsive, and who do not follow important rules at home, at school, or in the community. A number of different types of Behavioral Parent Training have been found effective, including Parent-Child Interaction Therapy, Incredible Years, and Parent Management Training. The therapist will work with you directly to help you apply these parenting strategies to your child.

Consult with your child's pediatrician about your child's behavior. That doctor may, in turn, refer your child to a developmental pediatrician (a pediatrician who specializes in behavior and developmental problems) or a psychiatrist. If your child has ADHD, a number of medication choices can be used as well. The medication you use should help your child focus his attention and help reduce his need to act impulsively. Medication should *not* change your child's core personality or make him or her "zombie"-like. If these changes occur, the dose is likely too high. In that case, you should immediately contact your child's prescribing physician.

Should We Have Family Therapy or Group Therapy?

Therapy with individual families and group-therapy approaches have both been found helpful in reducing sexual behavior problems in children. Treatments that work only with the child (and do not directly involve the caregivers) are not useful in reducing sexual behavior problems. Family therapy and group therapy have different advantages and disadvantages.

Family therapy
- can address complex, concurrent issues;
- can provide individualized treatment;
- may more readily address crises when they occur; and
- may be the only thing available, particularly in small, rural communities where therapy in a group would feel too threatening and too exposing to group members.

> "Having a child with sexual behavior problems can feel very isolating. While parents can often talk with other parents about things like poor grades, stealing, and fighting, sexual matters and sexual behavior problems are topics other parents just don't know how to take. It has been helpful to be with a group of parents who know the road I've been walking."
>
> —Parent of a 12-year-old boy
>
> "The group helped me know that other kids have the same problems and that there are people willing to help. I'm not alone."
>
> —Parent of 4-, 5-, and 6-year-old girls

Group therapy
- is the most common format for directly addressing sexual behavior problems;
- provides children with the opportunity to practice good skills with other children;
- provides an opportunity to be accountable to other children, since school-age children tend to look to other children for guidance;
- provides important support for the caregivers; and
- requires that the therapist maintains good control of the children's group. If the group is out of control, the benefits to the group are lessened.

When Do Children with Sexual Behavior Problems Require Inpatient or Residential Treatment?

Most children with sexual behavior problems can be treated on an outpatient basis while living at home. When children have sexually acted out with their younger brother or sister, they may temporarily need to live with a relative or in another home. Most of the time, children can be successfully raised at home with outpatient treatment, and without the removal of any children from the home. This option is discussed in more detail on pages 61–65.

Residential and inpatient treatment has downsides including cost, difficulty of maintaining caregiver involvement in treatment (due to transportation/distance issues), exposure to other children with severe problems, labeling, and stigma. These concerns have to be weighed against the potential benefits of residential care.

Residential and inpatient treatment should be reserved for the most severe cases, such as children with

- intense psychiatric disorders, such as psychotic symptoms (like hearing voices);
- highly aggressive or coercive sexual behavior that recurs despite appropriate outpatient treatment and close supervision;
- suicidal tendencies that include specific plans; and
- specific plans to physically harm others.

Children with any of the above characteristics should be evaluated by a qualified mental health professional to determine the need for a higher level of care, such as inpatient or residential placement.

Qualifications of Therapists

Children with sexual behavior problems should be seen by a licensed mental health professional who has

- child development expertise (including sexual development expertise);
- knowledge of the different types of childhood mental health disorders;
- familiarity with children who have multiple diagnoses, which is often the case with children with sexual behavior problems. The professional should be trained in the topics of ADHD, child

maltreatment, child trauma, and conditions that affect self-control;
- an understanding that larger social problems have an impact on children's behavior, including their sexual behavior;
- knowledge of current research and effective approaches for treating childhood mental health disorders and sexual behavior problems; and
- knowledge of the many cultural variations that exist in parenting and childhood sexual behavior.

SIX

Taking Action: Advocating for Children with Sexual Behavior Problems

No single state or federal agency manages children with sexual behavior problems. Sometimes child protective services (or child welfare) are involved. Sometimes law enforcement is involved. Some states have other agencies who oversee cases of children with sexual behavior problems. Each state has different regulations, policies, and rules for governing how it will address cases of children who have demonstrated such problems. The information below provides general guidelines regarding these agencies.

Child Protective Services

Every state in the union has child abuse and neglect reporting laws as well as Child Protective Services that are required to investigate suspected abuse and to protect children. Many children with sexual behavior problems, particularly preschool-age children, have experienced trauma, including child abuse. First and foremost, these children must be protected from further harm. Child Protective Services are provided by the state and are charged with protecting children from child maltreatment, including child sexual abuse, physical abuse, neglect, and emotional abuse. For children who are American Indian or Alaska Native, Indian Child Welfare is required to be involved in child protective matters.

In most states, child protective services address child abuse and neglect by a caregiver. In general (but it differs by state and jurisdiction), child protective services will investigate cases in which a child has demonstrated a sexual behavior problem when:

- there is reason to suspect that one or more children involved in the sexual behavior may have also been abused by a caregiver;
- a caregiver has been aware of the sexual behavior problems and has not taken protective actions to prevent future sexual behaviors;
- a child with sexual behavior problems needs appropriate treatment, and the caregiver fails to enroll and participate in such services (particularly when the youth has demonstrated aggressive, coercive, and/or repeated sexual behavior problems); and
- the caregiver is not providing appropriate protection and safety measures, due to such things as substance abuse or domestic violence.

In these cases, Child Protective Services will conduct an assessment or an investigation. An assessment is designed to identify service needs of the family and link them with supports. An investigation is initiated in the more severe or risky cases, and is designed to determine if abuse or neglect has occurred so that needed safety measures can be taken. Assessments and investigations often include interviews of the children, caregivers, and other involved adults. The investigation may also include an assessment of the safety and risk factors in the home environment.

Some jurisdictions use child-advocacy centers to conduct interviews with the children. Child-advocacy centers are child-friendly environments and have specially trained interviewers who typically work in conjunction with child protective services, law enforcement, and district attorneys.

The results of the investigation and child protective services' response can vary depending on the case, situation, and jurisdiction. Possible results and responses may determine one or more of the following:

- Child abuse and neglect are not confirmed, but services are recommended. A specific treatment program may be recommended by child protective services.
- The children involved in the sexual behavior problems were themselves victims of child abuse. If

so, safety measures will be required. If the person who was the abuser is in the home (such as the father, the aunt, or someone else), that person may be required to leave the residence. Another option is that the child may be placed in foster care or in a kinship care home.

- The caregiver "failed to protect" the children involved. These are cases in which child protective services believe that a caregiver knew about the sexual behavior problems or other risky situations and failed to act to protect the child. Responses can range from close monitoring and requiring services to the removal of the children from the home and the placement of the children in protective custody. Sometimes the state/Child Protective Services may remove all the children. At other times, just the child with the sexual behavior problems will be required to live in a home separate from his/her siblings. The caregiver would then be given a treatment plan to complete, to demonstrate that the caregiver has the capability to protect the children.
- The caregiver was neglectful when failing to find and participate in needed mental health or behavioral health services for a child with sexual behavior problems. If the caregiver is required to follow through with services, but fails to, the child may be removed from that adult's care and placed elsewhere to receive the required services.

Having Child Protective Services involved with your family can be somewhat intimidating, due in part to your level of uncertainty about what could happen. But the service's goal is the same as your goal, which is to keep your children safe from harm. With education, advocacy, and support, a partnership can be developed with Child Protective Services to help your children. Here are some recommendations to help with this process:

- Advocate that your children and family receive the types of treatment found to be most effective (see chapter 5).
- Develop a support network that will provide a safety team for your children and provide you with emotional support.
- Directly address any personal matters that would interfere with your ability to provide the types of supervision and parenting your children need, such as treatment for depression, substance abuse, or violence in the home or community.
- Advocate that all caregivers provide a safe and caring environment that meets the needs of the child or children.
- Advocate for a lawyer who knows your child's rights and understands and supports the best interests of your children and you.
- Communicate regularly with the Child Protective Services worker assigned to your family. If you have problems with communication with that person, contact the worker's supervisor.
- If you disagree with the findings of the Child Protective Services investigation, you can appeal. Every state is required to have an appeals process for caregivers.

Legal System

The legal system may become involved with families of children with sexual behavior problems in a variety of ways. If Child Protective Services are involved and confirm child abuse or neglect, then the children and caregivers will likely be involved in the court system. States refer to this court with different names, but often it is called Family Court. Cases involving Child Protective Services are often called "deprived," and a treatment plan for the family will be issued through the court. The family will be seen in court in front of the judge periodically (perhaps monthly, or every three or six months) until enough progress has been made that the case can be closed.

The legal system can also be involved with families of children with sexual behavior problems through law enforcement and juvenile services. This involvement may happen in cases where older youths (such as 11- or 12-year-olds) act out sexually with much younger children, particularly in cases where force, coercion, or aggression is used or in cases where the sexual behavior is explicit and intrusive (such as intercourse). In these cases, law enforcement may conduct an investigation that involves the interviewing of all children and adults potentially involved in the situation. Law enforcement will also conduct examinations of the scene or collect other evidence. States can charge juveniles with sexual offenses, but each state differs with regard to the age group to which juvenile statutes apply. Some states have applied juvenile statutes to children as young as 7 years old, but states more typically have an age limit of no less than 10 years of age.

After finding that a youth has committed a sexual offense, the legal system may respond to these cases in one of the following ways:

- postponing charging the child if the youth participates in services, and then dropping charges upon completion of the program;
- charging the child with a sexual offense, placing the child on probation, and requiring service participation; or
- charging the child with a sexual offense and placing the child in a juvenile facility.

Some states are now placing youths (mostly older youths) with sexual-offense histories on registries. More information about these registries is provided at www.ncsby.org/pages/registry.htm, a site that also includes a directory of all the states' statutes. It is important for caregivers to educate themselves about the registry laws in their own state. The Task Force Committee on Children with Sexual Behavior Problems from the Association for the Treatment of Sexual Abusers reports that registering children and publicly labeling them as sex offenders for life puts the children themselves at risk of significant harm that can range from educational discrimination and rejection to ostracism and vigilantism. No broad public protection is provided by the registration of children because children with sexual behavior problems simply are not a high-risk group, especially if provided with appropriate treatment. The full report of the Task Force can be found on the publications page of their Web site (www.atsa.com).

Can Children Who Have Had Sexual Behavior Problems Attend School with Other Children?

Most children who have had sexual behavior problems can attend public schools and participate in school activities without putting the safety of other students at risk. Children with serious, aggressive sexual behaviors—who are unresponsive to outpatient treatment and supervision—may need a more restrictive environment.

In some cases, school personnel may need to know information for safety and protection issues. When the sexual behavior has occurred in school settings, where the child is assessed to be at high risk or where the serious sexual behavior continues, it is appropriate to notify school personnel. When school personnel are notified, we recommend that accurate information be provided in addition to concrete recommendations. For example, recommendations for teachers may include changing bathroom breaks so that the child can use the bathroom alone. The recommendations should also include the provision of additional supervision during the more unstructured times (such as at recess and lunchtime). Notifying other children or children's parents at the school is unnecessary. Such notifications may have a negative impact on the child, potentially causing the child to be isolated from or rejected by peers. Alerting school personnel regarding sexual behavior problems is not always necessary, particularly when the child's sexual behavior has not occurred in the school settings, when the child is currently receiving treatment for his sexual behavior problems, or when the behavior doesn't happen often, or is not ongoing.

SEVEN

Placement and Reunification

Can Children with Sexual Behavior Problems Live with Other Children?

With appropriate treatment and careful supervision, most children with sexual behavior problems can live safely with other children. The safety and well-being of *all* the children should be evaluated when making decisions about where children should live. Placement is not determined by a single factor. Instead, a number of factors need to be evaluated for placement decisions. These factors include

- how well the caregivers can provide close visual supervision and can respond to the needs of all the children;
- what safety measures can be added to the home environment to increase the level of supervision and safety (for example, sleeping arrangements may need to be changed);
- whether or not the child has demonstrated sexual behavior problems with his or her siblings or other children in the home. In those cases, the reactions and responses of the other children need to be assessed; and
- how severe the child's sexual behavior problems are and how well the child is responding to supervision and treatment. Children with highly aggressive or intrusive sexual behavior, despite treatment and close supervision, should not live with other young children until this behavior is resolved.

All the children can often remain in the home environment when a caregiver understands and is capable of providing the needed supervision and oversight, when the child responds to supervision and parenting strategies with reduced sexual behavior problems, and when the other children want to remain with their sibling and do not have strong feelings of fear or anxiety.

Alternative placements will need to be found when a caregiver is incapable of providing supervision (due to something like an addiction to drugs), when the child continues to demonstrate repeated, aggressive sexual behavior problems despite supervision, or when other children are experiencing significant distress about continuing to live with the child who acted out sexually. Ideally, caregivers in the alternative placements will

- be actively involved in effective treatment services;
- provide the least restrictive environment that also provides the needed safety measures;
- be part of the natural community of the youth and the youth's family;
- limit the number of other changes in the child's life (such as school placement or after-school activities); and
- be involved in the plan to transition the child back to his/her home environment as soon as possible with appropriate safety measures and consideration of the well-being of all the children involved.

Decisions regarding exactly when to return children with sexual behavior problems to their homes and to their parents and siblings are largely based on the same factors. It can only happen when the caregiver is capable of providing the right parenting, the child is responding to supervision and outpatient treatment, and the siblings are responsive to living together with the child again.

Such a reunification process must be individualized. Steps to enhance the success of the reunification include:

1. The caregiver's direct involvement in the treatment of all the children.
2. The existence of well-developed supervision and safety plans with the caregiver and the children. The safety plan should be discussed with the entire family. The members must agree, understand, and be capable of following the plan (suggestions for safety plans are provided below).
3. The holding of meetings with family members to discuss the safety plan and the transition home.
4. Visits in the home, in natural family situations, with increasing frequency and duration as the children and caregivers successfully implement the safety plan.
5. The child's move back home, with continuing involvement and support provided by the behavior-health provider/therapist for all family members.

Components of the Safety Plan

Safety plans are more likely to be needed with older children who have had aggressive or coercive sexual behavior problems. The safety plan includes

- rules for the children;
- activities the children can do and are encouraged to be able to do;
- responsibilities of the caregivers in charge of the children in the home; and
- the family's rules regarding privacy and supervision.

The following provides a framework for developing a safety plan. A qualified professional will assist in individualizing the plan for the family circumstances.

Rules for the Children

My child _____ will learn and obey these rules:
1. Will not babysit for any amount of time.
2. Will not go into his/her brothers' and sisters' bedrooms without adult supervision. If he/she is invited into one of their bedrooms, the child will say, "No."
3. Will not have his/her brothers or sisters come into his/her bedroom, unless an adult is notified and is in the room to keep an eye on things.
4. Will not be in the bathroom if one of his/her brothers or sisters is in there. (Only one person can go into the bathroom at a time.)
5. Will keep the bathroom door closed when in there.
6. Will not engage in any "horseplay," wrestling, or tickling with brothers, sisters, or any other young children.
7. Will not to watch any movies, TV shows, or Internet material or listen to music that his/her parents have not approved.
8. Will not talk about sexual things or make any sexual comments or sexual jokes around his/her brothers, sisters, or other children.
9. Will not be alone with other children.

Some things my child *can* do at home—if it's OK with her brothers, sisters, and parents—are:
1. Watch TV, read, listen to music, or play sports or games with his/her brothers and sisters.
2. Sit next to brothers or sisters on the couch.
3. Talk and joke politely with brothers and sisters.
4. Go to church, to the store, or on family outings with the family.
5. Ride in the car with the family.
6. Eat meals or go to restaurants with the family.
7. Show appropriate affection to brothers and sisters if the brothers/sisters initiate it and *if* one of the parents is there to watch. Hugs are often OK.

Rules for the Family

I, as the caregiver, agree to:
1. Supervise interactions between my child and all other involved children, including brothers and sisters.
2. Not ask my child to babysit.
3. Make sure that an informed, responsible adult is always in charge of the children.
4. Supervise TV shows, music, videos, and Internet material.
5. Monitor my child's activities, such as school work, homework, types of friends, and whereabouts, etc., and help my child make good choices.
6. Help my child to follow the rules by reminding him/her about them, if he/she needs it.
7. Make sure that all the children are clothed unless they are in their own room with the door closed, in the bathroom with the door closed, or in bed.
8. Be open and accepting when talking with my child about any sexual questions or thoughts he/she might have.

The family agrees to:
1. Treat each other with respect.
2. Respect the authority of the parents/caregivers and follow their house rules.
3. Listen to each other.
4. Be kind to each other.
5. Dress respectfully.
6. Have fun activities with each other.
7. Provide individual time for each child to talk privately with parents about important matters, including questions about relationships.
8. Help each other to be successful and to follow the rules of the family.

The family is encouraged to develop and individualize its safety plan with the guidance of a behavioral-health professional.

EIGHT

Taking Action: Taking Care of Yourself

Raising a child who has sexually acted out with another child can be quite stressful for caregivers. In addition, many of these youths have been traumatized, adding to the complexity and concern for the children. Of the hundreds of families for whom we have provided services, most of the caregivers are so focused on supporting and caring for their children that they forget how important it is to take care of themselves, too. Your children need you to take care of yourself. You are their role model. If you don't take care of yourself, they can't learn how to be healthy people. If you don't take care of yourself, your energy will be taxed, which may impact your ability to parent well. You will be a better caregiver if you have the mental, physical, emotional, and spiritual energy to meet the needs of the children in your care. It is important for you and your children that you

- eat a healthy diet;
- get enough sleep;
- do something enjoyable for yourself on a regular basis (such as sports, crafts, painting, or socializing);
- exercise regularly;
- create time with other adults during which you can talk about concerns you might have, without your children in earshot (they have radar!);
- have a support system;
- don't turn to alcohol or drugs when under stress;
- have a way to deal with stress that is healthy for you;
- identify family members and/or friends who can provide support; and
- find supportive adults in the community, such as

at local faith communities, neighborhood groups, or community agencies.

Parenting is hard. Children do not come with a manual or rule book to let you know how to raise them. Children are a delight and can make each day special, but sometimes, life becomes so hectic and stressed that we fail to recognize this fact. If you have tried to adhere to the above list, but still find that informal supports are not enough, seek professional supports such as the following:

- Parenting support groups
- Parent education programs
- Systems of Care (an organization designed to help families with children who have multiple needs; the organization helps identify and coordinate financial, mental health, physical health, and other supports for the family)
- Individual therapy
- Family therapy
- Medications (such as antidepressants)
- Substance abuse services
- Domestic violence shelters and services

As a caregiver for a child with sexual behavior problems, you are taking the first important steps to help your child and all of your family. By reading this booklet, you have given yourself a foundation of knowledge about sexual development and sexual behavior problems, and you have learned ways to prevent future sexual behavior problems. Remember, you are not alone. Effective treatments to reduce your child's future risk are available for you.

RESOURCES

Below are lists of Web sites and books that address topics discussed in this booklet. These are resources that families and team members have found helpful over the years. The resources vary in regards to the topic areas as well as in the values emphasized. Parents and caregivers are advised to examine multiple resources to find the ones that best fit the needs of their family.

Web Sites

Child Sexual Abuse Prevention

Stop It Now!
  www.stopitnow.org
  www.safersociety.org (distributor of Stop It Now! books)
  Offering tools to adults, families, and communities to protect children from abuse before it happens.

Child Sexual Abuse

The National Child Traumatic Stress Network
  www.nctsnet.org
  Providing the resources for improved care and services for families of children with traumatic stress.

Child Sexual Behavior Problems including Assessment and Treatment

The Association for the Treatment of Sexual Abusers
  www.atsa.com
  A nonprofit whose mission is to promote research and professional education, and to facilitate information exchange for successful treatment of sexual offenders.

National Center on Sexual Behavior of Youth
  www.ncsby.org
  A Center developed by the Office of Juvenile Justice and Delinquency Prevention and the Center on Child Abuse and Neglect, University of Oklahoma Health Sciences Center providing information and support for children with sexual behavior problems and adolescents with illegal sexual behavior.

Communicating with Youth about Sexual Matters

Advocates for Youth
www.advocatesforyouth.org
Offering a positive and realistic approach to adolescent sexual heath, with education that empowers youth to make informed and responsible decisions for their sexual health.

4Parents.gov
Government site for parents with tips for talking to children, preteens, and teens about healthy and safe sexual behavior choices.

Talking with Kids about Tough Issues
www.talkingwithkids.org
Part of NBC's award-winning campaign, The More You Know, offers tips for parents when talking to kids about difficult issues ranging from abuse to terrorism.

Media Impact

American Psychological Association Online
"American Psychological Association's (APA) Task Force Report on the Sexualization of Girls"
www.apa.org/pi/wpo/sexualization.html
APA's report on the consequences of the media on girls.

Trauma

The National Child Traumatic Stress Network
www.nctsnet.org
Providing the resources for improved care and services for families of children with traumatic stress.

Books

Annunziata, J., and M. Nemiroff. 2003. *Sex and babies: First facts.* Washington, DC: Magination Press.

Brohl, K., and J. C. Potter. 2004. *When your child has been molested: A parent's guide to healing and recovery.* Revised edition. San Francisco: Jossey-Bass.

Brown, L. K., and M. Brown. 1997. *What's the big secret? Talking about sex with girls and boys.* Boston: Little, Brown and Company.

Colblentz, J. 1992. *God's will for my body; Guidance for adolescents.* Harrisonburg, VA: Christian Light Publications, Inc.

Girard, L. W. 1984. *My body is private.* Morton Grove: Albert Whitman & Company.

Gravelle, K., N. Castro, and C. Castro. 1998. *What's going on down there? Answers to questions boys find hard to ask.* New York: Walker and Company.

Gravelle, K., and J. Gravelle. 1996. *The period book: Everything you don't want to ask (But need to know).* New York: Walker and Company.

Haffner, D. W. 1999. *From diapers to dating: A parent's guide to raising sexually healthy children.* New York: Newmarket Press.

Hagans, K. B., and J. Case. 1988. *When your child has been molested: A parent's guide to healing and recovery.* New York: Lexington Books.

Harris, R. H. 1994. *Changing bodies, growing up, sex and sexual health; It's perfectly normal.* Cambridge: Candlewick Press.

———. 2002. *It's so amazing! A book about eggs, sperm, birth, babies, and families (ages 7 and up).* Cambridge: Candlewick Press.

———. *It's not the stork; A book about girls, boys, babies, bodies, families, and friends.* Cambridge: Candlewick Press.

Harris, R. H., and M. Emberley. 1996. *It's perfectly normal: Changing bodies, growing up, sex, and sexual health.* Cambridge, MA: Candlewick Press.

Herrerias, C. 1996. *Teen to teen: A personal safety and sexual abuse prevention.* Charlotte, NC: Kidsrights Inc.

Johnson, T. C. 1999. *Understanding child's sexual behavior: What's natural and healthy.* Oakland, CA: New Harbinger Publications.

Jones, S., and B. Jones. 1995. *What's the big deal? Why God cares about sex (ages 8 – 11).* Colorado Springs: Navpress Books & Bible Studies.

Lasser, M. 1999. *Talking to your kids about sex; How to have a lifetime of age-appropriate conversations with your children about healthy sexuality.* Colorado Springs: WaterBrook Press.

Leman, K., and K. F. Bell. 2004. *A chicken's guide to talking turkey with your kids about sex.* Grand Rapids: Zondervan.

Madaras, L. 2003. *Ready, set, grow! A "what's happening to my body?" Book for younger girls.* New York: Newmarket Press.

Madaras, L. and A. Madaras. 2000. *The what's happening to my body? Book for boys. A growing up guide for parents and sons.* New York: Newmarket Press.

Marsh, C. S. 1998. *Sex stuff for kids: A book of practical information and ideas for kids 7-17.* Atlanta: Carole Marsh/Gallopade.

Mayle, P. 1975. *"What's happening to me?" An illustrated guide to puberty.* New York: Kensington Publishing Corp.

———. 2000. *"Where did I come from?" A guide for children and parents.* New York: Kensington Publishing Corp.

Richardson, J., and M. A. Schuster. 2003. *Everything you never wanted your kids to know about sex (but were afraid they'd ask).* New York: Crown Publishers.

Royston, A. 1996. *Where do babies come from?* New York: DK Publishing.

Schaefer, V., and N. Bendell. 1998. *The care and keeping of you: The body book for girls*. Middleton, WI: Pleasant Company Publications.

Schwartz, P., and D. Cappello. 2000. *Ten talks parents must have with their children about sex and character*. New York: Hyperion.

Stauffer, L. 1999. *Let's talk about safety skills for kids. A personal safety activity book for parents and children*. Hatfield, PA: Hope for Families, Inc.

Stauffer, L., and E. Deblinger. 1999. *Let's talk about taking care of you! An educational book about body safety*. Hatfield, PA: Hope for Families, Inc.

Stoppard, M. 1997. *Sex ed: Growing up, relationships, and sex*. New York: DK Publishing.

ABOUT THE AUTHOR

JANE F. SILOVSKY, Ph.D., is a clinical child psychologist and the associate director of the Center on Child Abuse and Neglect. Dr. Silovsky received her doctorate in clinical psychology from the University of Alabama. Currently, she is an associate professor in the Department of Pediatrics at the University of Oklahoma Health Sciences Center. Since 1997 she has been the director of the Children with Sexual Behavior Problems Program, an assessment, treatment, and research program for preschool and school-age children with sexual behavior problems. Dr. Silovsky's research is in the area of treatment outcome and program evaluation of services for children affected by child maltreatment. She has published research on preschool and school-age children with sexual behavior problems.